What Is an Insect?

Molly Aloian

Crabtree Publishing Company
www.crabtreebooks.com

Author
Molly Aloian

Publishing plan research and development
Reagan Miller, Crabtree Publishing Company

Editorial director
Kathy Middleton

Editor
Crystal Sikkens

Proofreader
Kelley McNiven

Indexer
Wendy Scavuzzo

Design
Samara Parent

Photo research
Crystal Sikkens, Samara Parent

**Production coordinator
and prepress technician**
Samara Parent

Print coordinator
Margaret Amy Salter

Photographs
BrandXPictures: page 18 (right)
Dreamstime: pages 15, 19
Thinkstock: page 20 (right)
Wikimedia Commons: Waugsberg: page 21
All other images by Shutterstock

Library and Archives Canada Cataloguing in Publication

Aloian, Molly, author
      What is an insect? / Molly Aloian.

(Insects close-up)
Includes index.
Issued in print and electronic formats.
ISBN 978-0-7787-1279-4 (bound).--ISBN 978-0-7787-1283-1 (pbk.).--
ISBN 978-1-4271-9365-0 (pdf).--ISBN 978-1-4271-9361-2 (html)

      1. Insects--Juvenile literature. I. Title.

QL467.2.A564 2013   j595.7   C2013-904048-X
                                                          C2013-904049-8

Library of Congress Cataloging-in-Publication Data

Aloian, Molly.
      What is an insect? / Molly Aloian.
        p. cm. -- (Insects close-up)
      Includes index.
      ISBN 978-0-7787-1279-4 (reinforced library binding) -- ISBN 978-0-7787-
1283-1 (pbk.) -- ISBN 978-1-4271-9365-0 (electronic pdf) -- ISBN 978-1-4271-
9361-2 (electronic html)
      1. Insects--Juvenile literature. I. Title. II. Series: Aloian, Molly. Insects close-
up.

QL467.2.A447 2013
595.7--dc23
                                          2013023439

Crabtree Publishing Company

www.crabtreebooks.com   1-800-387-7650

Printed in Hong Kong/092013/BK20130703

**Published in Canada
Crabtree Publishing**
616 Welland Ave.
St. Catharines, Ontario
L2M 5V6

**Published in the United States
Crabtree Publishing**
PMB 59051
350 Fifth Avenue, 59th Floor
New York, New York 10118

**Published in the United Kingdom
Crabtree Publishing**
Maritime House
Basin Road North, Hove
BN41 1WR

**Published in Australia
Crabtree Publishing**
3 Charles Street
Coburg North
VIC 3058

Contents

An insect is an animal

An insect is a type of animal. There are many kinds of insects. Some insects are tiny. Others are big. Insects are also different shapes and colors.

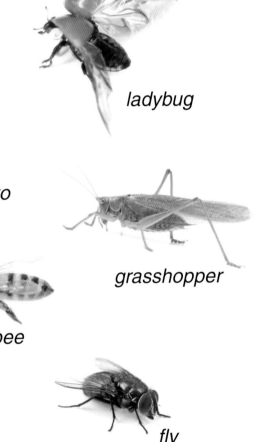
ladybug

mosquito

grasshopper

bee

praying
mantis

fly

Insects that fly

Most insects have wings. They use their wings to fly from place to place. Some insects do not have wings. They crawl or jump from place to place.

butterfly

cockroach

dragonfly

What do you think?

Look at the insects on these pages. All of these insects have wings. Can you find their wings?

An invertebrate

An insect is an **invertebrate**. An invertebrate is an animal that does not have a **backbone**. A backbone is a group of bones down the middle of an animal's back. Instead of a backbone, an insect has a hard covering over its body. This hard covering is called an **exoskeleton**.

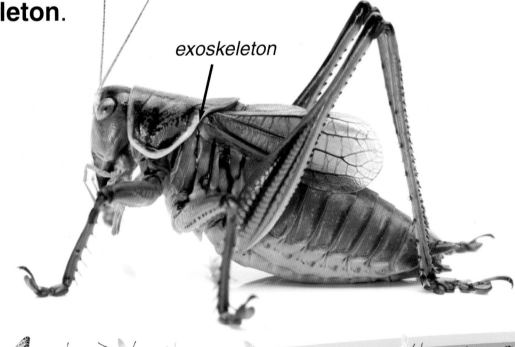

exoskeleton

Covered up

The exoskeleton covers an insect's whole body. It even covers its legs and head. It helps protect the insect from **predators**. Predators are animals that hunt and eat other animals. Plenty of animals like to eat insects!

An exoskeleton protects the insect's body underneath from getting wet.

One, two, three

An insect's body has three main sections. It has a head, a **thorax**, and an **abdomen**.

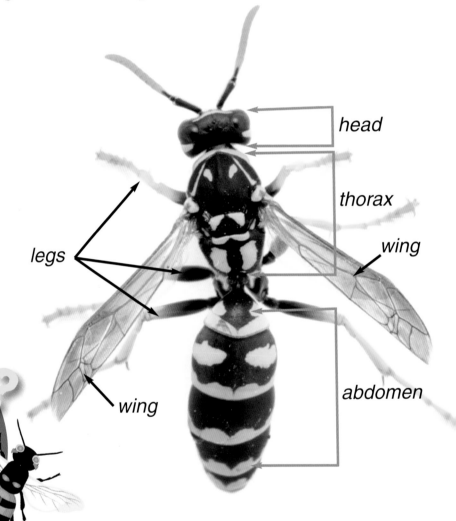

head

thorax

wing

legs

wing

abdomen

What do you think?

Which section are an insect's wings attached to?

8

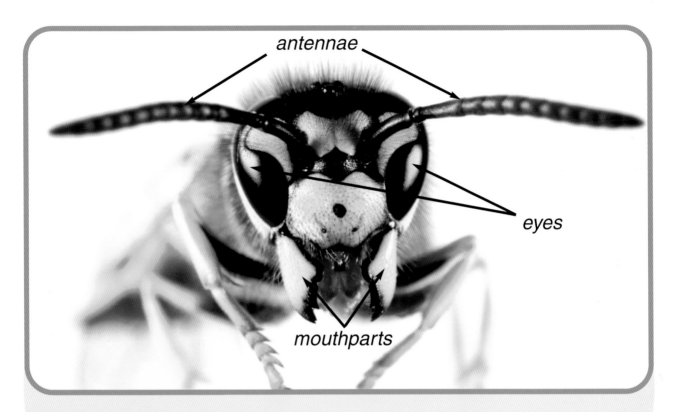

antennae

eyes

mouthparts

Body parts

An insect's eyes and **mouthparts** are on its head. There are also two feelers called **antennae** on an insect's head. All insects have six legs that are attached to their thorax. An insect's **organs** are inside its abdomen.

On the move

Insects use their legs and wings to move. All insects have legs that bend, just like your legs bend. Having legs that bend help insects move quickly from place to place. Insects use their legs to run, jump, and swim.

What do you think?

Would the ant in this picture be able to fly off the branch? Why or why not?

Ants use their legs to climb.

Fly by

Most insects have wings. Some have one pair of wings. Others have two pairs of wings. Insects flap their wings quickly to fly from place to place. They can fly to get away from hungry predators.

Flies have one pair of wings.

Dragonflies have two pairs of wings.

Where do insects live?

Insects live all over the world. They live in **habitats** such as swamps, forests, deserts, and even underground. Their habitats provide the insects with the food, water, and shelter they need to stay alive.

A mosquito is a common insect found in swamp habitats.

Home sweet home

Insects find homes in their habitats. Some insects live in small spaces between rocks or plants. Other insects make their homes. Many insects dig **burrows** into the ground. Others build **hives** or nests. Their homes keep them safe from predators and sheltered from bad weather.

Bees build homes called hives.

Termites build large nests out of dirt called **mounds**.

Insect food

Different insects eat different foods. They find these foods in their habitats. Some insects eat plants. They might eat roots, bark, leaves, stems, or drink **nectar**. Nectar is a sweet liquid found in flowers. Insects that eat plants are called **herbivores**.

These longhorn beetles are eating a leaf off a plant.

Eating other animals

Other insects eat animals. They might eat snails, worms, millipedes, or even other insects. Insects that eat animals are called **carnivores**.

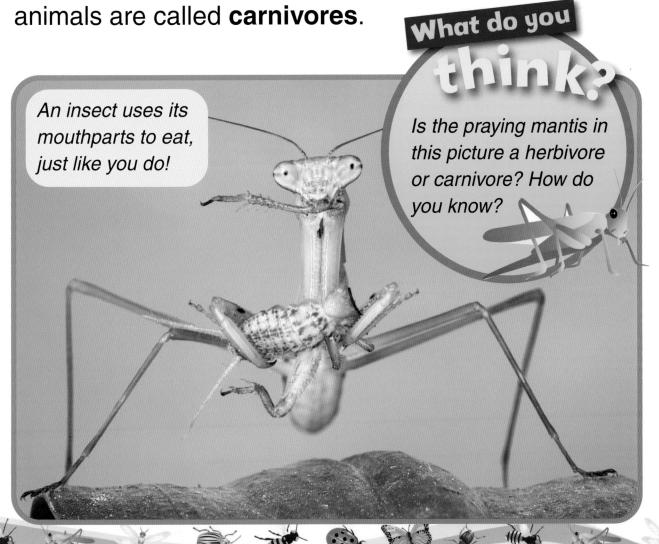

An insect uses its mouthparts to eat, just like you do!

What do you **think?**

Is the praying mantis in this picture a herbivore or carnivore? How do you know?

Baby to adult

Insects go through many changes as they grow from babies to adults. The changes are called **metamorphosis**. Many baby insects go through four stages of metamorphosis.

Once these baby rhinoceros beetles go through metamorphosis, they will look like the adult below.

Big changes

Adult insects lay eggs. A **larva** hatches from an egg. Many larvae grow until they are big enough to form a case around themselves. The insect then becomes a **pupa**. Inside the case it changes into its adult form. The adult then breaks out of the case when it is fully grown.

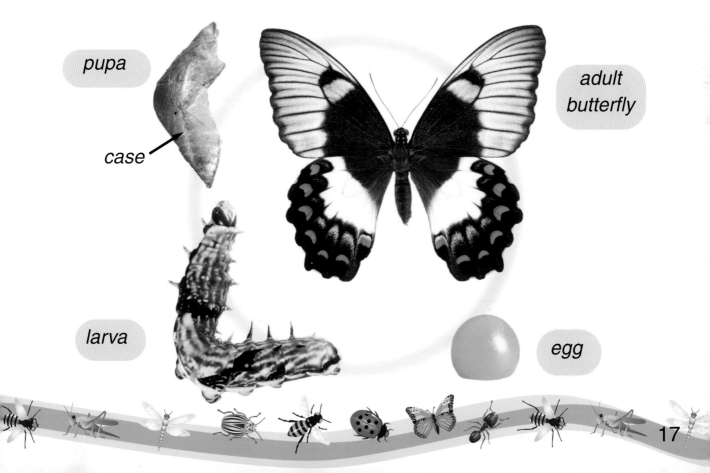

pupa

case

adult butterfly

larva

egg

Not an insect

Many people think a spider is an insect, but it is not. An insect is different from a spider. A spider has eight legs. An insect has six legs. Many insects have wings. Spiders do not have wings.

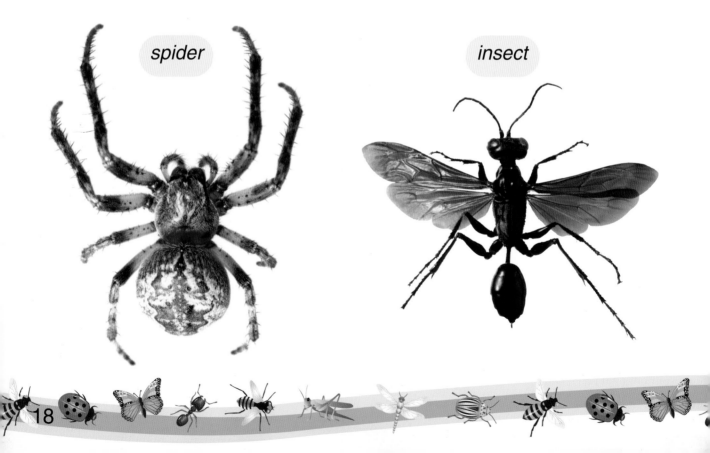

spider

insect

Different bodies

An insect has three main body sections. A spider has only two. A baby insect goes through metamorphosis. A baby spider does not.

This baby spider looks just like the adult spider only smaller.

What do you think?

Do insect larvae, or babies, look the same as adults? Why or why not?

Insects are important!

More than half of all the animals on Earth are insects! Insects are important because they are food for many other animals. Spiders, scorpions, bats, birds, and frogs are just some of the animals that eat insects.

Can you tell which insects this lizard and bird are about to eat?

Pollen for plants

Insects also help plants grow. Some plants need **pollen** from other plants to make seeds. Insects, such as bees and butterflies, move pollen from one plant to another. The plants can then make seeds and new plants can grow.

pollen

When a bee lands on a flower, pollen sticks to its body. The pollen then rubs off onto the next flower the bee lands on.

Insect hunt

This activity will help you discover insects in their natural habitats. Choose an area in your yard, in a park, or in another natural place. Look under rocks, near plants, and around trees. Look closely for insects and record what you find in a journal. Be careful not to touch the insects.

Answer the following questions in your journal:
What insects did I see?
How many insects were there?
What were the insects doing?
Did the insects have wings?

Learning more

Books

Schatz, Dennis. *Totally Bugs* (Totally Books).
    Silver Dolphin Books, 2013.

Dussling, Jennifer. *Bugs! Bugs! Bugs! (DK Readers).*
    DK Publishing, 2011.

Kalman, Bobbie. *The ABCs of Insects (ABCs of the Natural World).*
    Crabtree Publishing Company, 2009.

Kalman, Bobbie and Rebecca Sjonger. *Everyday Insects* (The World
    of Insects). Crabtree Publishing Company, 2006.

Websites

Fun Insect Facts for Kids—Interesting information about Insects
www.sciencekids.co.nz/sciencefacts/animals/insect.html

Let's Talk About Insects
http://urbanext.illinois.edu/insects/01.html

BBC Nature—All Insects
www.bbc.co.uk/nature/life/Insect/by/rank/all

Ladybug Facts and Pictures
http://kids.nationalgeographic.com/kids/animals/creaturefeature/ladybug/

Words to know

Note: Some boldfaced words are defined where they appear in the book.

antennae (an-TEN-ee) noun Feelers that help insects sense the world around them

burrows (BUR-ohs) noun Tunnels that are dug into the ground

habitats (HAB-i-tats) noun Natural places where animals live

hives (hahyvs) noun Places where bees and wasps live

larva (LAHR-vah) noun A baby insect that hatches from an egg

mouthparts (MOUTH-pahrts) noun Body parts that insects use to gather or eat food

organs (AWR-guhns) noun Parts of an animal's body, such as the heart or lungs, which do important jobs

pollen (POL-uhn) noun A powdery substance found in flowers that plants need to make seeds

pupa (PYOO-puh) noun A young insect that is changing from a larva to an adult

*A noun is a person, place, or thing.
An adjective is a word that tells you what something is like.
A verb is an action word that tells you what someone or something does.*

Index